This is a true story about Shogun, the Leonberger
and his pal Moon, the Golden Retriever.
They live with their Mum, Jane and Dad, Geoff in the
North Island of New Zealand.

© Jane Pordon, 2020

ISBN 978-0-473-53856-9

Hello, I'm Jane and I am Shogun's mum. When I first met a garden full of Leonbergers I instantly fell in love with them. These gentle, giant dogs are known for their love of people, especially children. They are very loyal, friendly dogs, have big tongues to give you lots of kisses and big fluffy tails to dry your face on afterwards!

Over the years I have had several Leonbergers. Jeep is my third Leo - as we call them for short - and he is now six years old. When he was just three, he told me he was a bit lonely and would love to have a four-legged friend to play with. I looked and looked for a baby Leo but just couldn't find one. Instead I managed to find a Golden Retriever puppy, I called him Moon, and at eight weeks old Moon came home to rule the roost.

Moon has grown up thinking he is a Leonberger. Jeep was always so gentle with him and, never told him off, so, at a young age Moon became the leader of the dog pack in this house! Jeep and Moon hated to be parted. Where one was the other was right behind. Soon after, Shogun came to live with us. He is Jeep's son.

Now Jeep is older and a little slower, he tends to sit and watch the youngsters play. It is Shogun who now dashes off with Moon, Moon still always in the lead, having the time of their lives around our property. Double trouble!

Oh, I have so many stories about their adventures I could write a book!

However, this time, I think I may need some help from Shogun, after all, I wasn't there for most of his adventure.

Hi, nice to meet you, my name is Shogun, I'm 19 months old now. I live in an old house with a huge garden. I live with my human mum and dad, my real doggy dad, Jeep, and my best pal Moon. Moon told me he's a Goldie and is the boss round here. I don't really understand why he thinks he's the boss, he's so little!

One day I got lost, our garden gate was left open by mistake. Moon, quick as a flash, ran out of the gate and raced off down the drive, calling for me to follow him. Of course, I followed him as he turned and dashed through next door's orchard. I didn't even look back to say goodbye to Mum as she whistled and whistled for us to come back. Oh boy this was going to be fun, going somewhere new on our own! What an adventure we were going to have.

Once we were through next door's small fruit orchard, we found our way into the next one. We were lucky that somebody had left that gate open too. This orchard was REALLY big. In fact, it was massive! Moon went down one row of trees and I went down another. The dead, brown and orange crunchy leaves crackled under my big feet. I always kept my eye on Moon though, I never really knew what he would do next, and I didn't want to get lost.

Occasionally we stopped to eat some old fruit that had been left on the ground. They were so yummy I could have stayed there for ages eating them, but Moon was on the move again, so off we went. For such a little dog he ran so fast I could hardly keep up with him. We ran like the wind.

In the middle of the orchard there were lots of trees and bushes, and I heard Moon shout, "I can smell water. Come on Shogun! Hurry up! We can go for a swim." He disappeared between two bushes and into the trees. "Oh, this is great fun," I thought to myself, and I followed him into the wood.

Once I got inside the wood. I got a little scared. It was quite dark, and I couldn't see the sky. The trees were so tall with lots of vines hanging down from them. There was thick, wiry ivy growing over the ground and up into the trees, and bushes with long strands of spikey bramble that kept getting caught in

the long hair on my legs. Old, gnarly tree stumps
and rotten branches that had fallen off the trees
kept tripping me up. Still, I had to follow Moon.
He was older than me after all, and the boss. I kept
going as best as I could, but the land kept getting
steeper and steeper. Oh dear me, it was so slippery
after all the rain we had had yesterday.

"NOOOOO!" and "HEEELP!" I shouted as I slipped and skidded down the steep bank. My legs got tangled in ivy and vines. I tumbled over one of the rotten branches and started rolling and spinning. I was so scared. Then I was falling, falling, falling. THUMP! "OOMPH!" I landed. It took me a few minutes to catch my breath, but, where was I?

I looked around me and all I could see was cold damp earth everywhere. I was in a big hole. It was very deep, and I couldn't see out of it, I could see the trees swaying in the breeze above me. I couldn't understand, why wasn't Moon in there too? I could hear him though, splashing around in the stream that was running through the ravine. If I jumped, I just managed to catch glimpses of him, rolling around in the water.

"Moon help me! " I cried "I'm stuck in this hole, I can't get out". But he just ignored me and kept playing in the water. He was running up and down the stream, in and out, making big splashes. He was having a wonderful time and I was stuck in this deep, dark, cold hole.

"OK", I thought, "maybe I can dig myself out." So, I started digging but it was tiring. I managed to get enough soil dug out of the side of the hole to make a little step. Ah, now I could stand on it and see Moon. He was filthy. That stream water was not very clean at all. It made him all black.

"Moon!" I called him again. "Please help me get out of here. I'm really stuck. Don't leave me here on my own. I'm scared. I don't like it in here."

Eventually Moon stopped splashing and enjoying himself and heard me calling him. "Don't worry Shogun I'm going for help," he said. He clambered up the steep side on the other side of the stream. Then he was gone - and I was all alone. What was I going to do?

It seemed like forever before I heard my mum and dad shouting my name and I could smell my doggy dad Jeep who had been brought out to track for me. Jeep's very clever at finding things, and now he had found me, but it sounded like they were pulling him away from the edge. It was too steep and dangerous for them. They couldn't see me from where they stood, and I didn't know if I should call out or not. I thought I might get into trouble if I barked so I decided to stay quiet, and try to get out of there on my own.

I started to dig again; but after a while my paws became very tired. At least the step I had made to stand on was now big enough to sit on. So, I sat, and sat, and sat and waited! How much longer, I wondered, would I have to stay there? It was really starting to get cold now. Thank goodness I had such a big fluffy coat to help keep me warm. I was hungry and thirsty too. (my tummy always tells me when it's nearly teatime). Now I was getting really fed up and decided that next time I heard anybody calling my name I would answer them as loudly as I could. I just couldn't go without my tea!

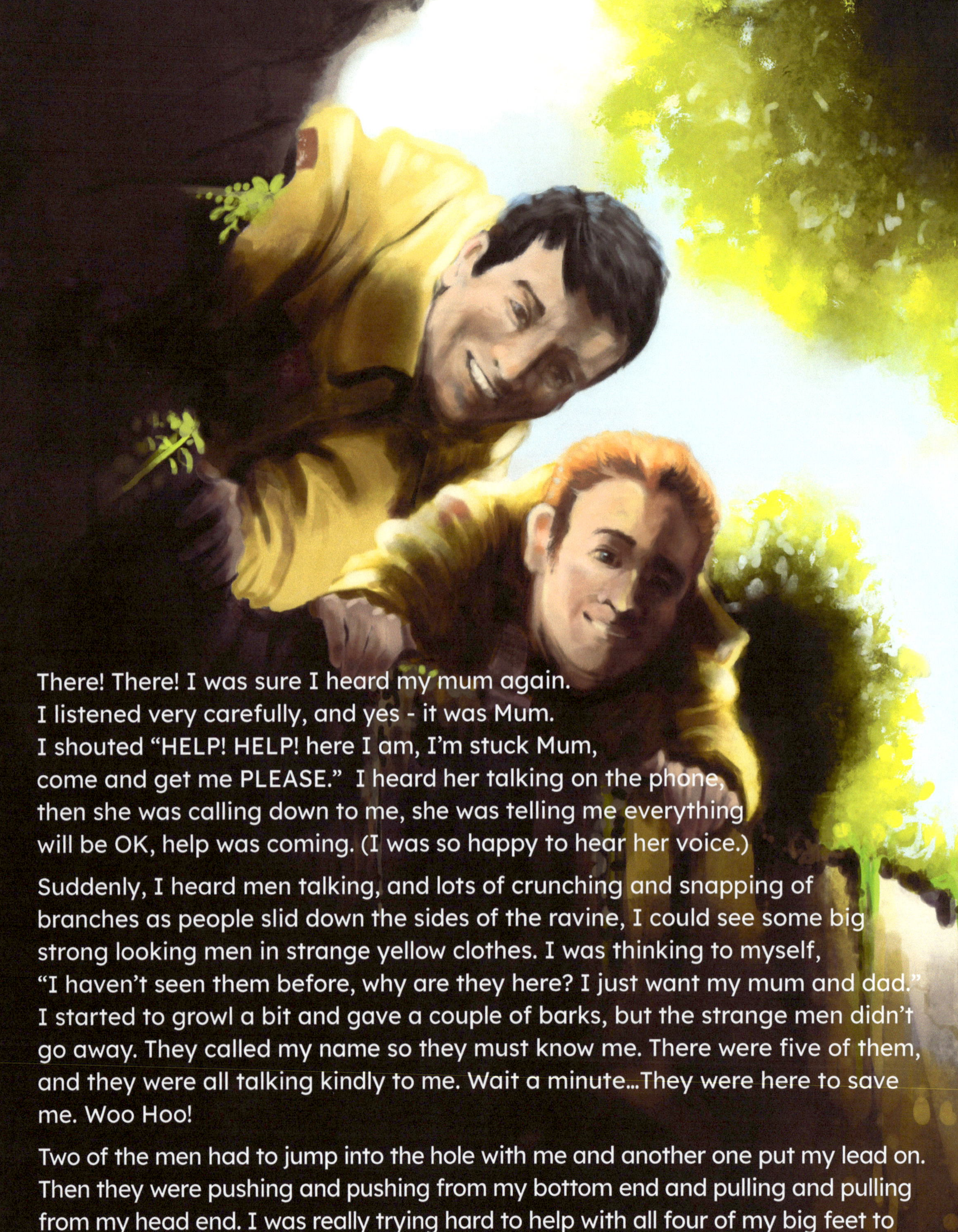

There! There! I was sure I heard my mum again.
I listened very carefully, and yes - it was Mum.
I shouted "HELP! HELP! here I am, I'm stuck Mum,
come and get me PLEASE." I heard her talking on the phone,
then she was calling down to me, she was telling me everything
will be OK, help was coming. (I was so happy to hear her voice.)

Suddenly, I heard men talking, and lots of crunching and snapping of
branches as people slid down the sides of the ravine, I could see some big
strong looking men in strange yellow clothes. I was thinking to myself,
"I haven't seen them before, why are they here? I just want my mum and dad."
I started to growl a bit and gave a couple of barks, but the strange men didn't
go away. They called my name so they must know me. There were five of them,
and they were all talking kindly to me. Wait a minute...They were here to save
me. Woo Hoo!

Two of the men had to jump into the hole with me and another one put my lead on.
Then they were pushing and pushing from my bottom end and pulling and pulling
from my head end. I was really trying hard to help with all four of my big feet to
scrabble up the side of the hole, but it was so slippery I just couldn't get a grip.

Slowly, slowly, with everyone pushing and pulling I got out of the
hole, then two more men helped pull me up the side of the ravine
back up through the wood and into the orchard.

Wow! those men were great getting me out of there, I was so happy
to be out of that horrible hole that I gave them all big sloppy kisses.
Then I saw my mum and I just knew everything was going to be alright.
I'd been saved!

I hate my photo being taken but the Te Puke firemen wanted a photo
of me, so Mum made me sit in front of them and she took a photo.
I didn't really mind as now these five men were my heroes.

Mum thought we should thank them again properly as she and Dad were so pleased to have me home safe and sound. A few days later we all piled into the car. Mum was carrying a huge chocolate cake and said I shouldn't go near it as chocolate was really bad for dogs and I would be very sick if I ate it… as if I would.

We went to Te Puke Fire Station on their training night, I was so pleased to
see my heroes again and they all seemed pleased to see me and were very
impressed with Jeep. I gave them lots of big licks to let them know how
grateful I was. Then me and Jeep did a lap of honour thanking all the fire
fighters for all they do, especially saving me. Te Puke Fire Fighters are the best!

We had to leave then as they were going to set the fire alarm off for practice
and I don't think I would have liked that!

Goodbye from Shogun until our next adventure.

Shogun in hot wate

Shogun with his rescuers, Karl Simmons (left), Dan Turner, Reece Jor Matt Atchison and Blair Reeves. Photo

This is the team from Te Puke Fire Brigade
who saved Shogun from the ravine.

Jeep, Shogun and Moon

Thank you for reading our true adventure story.

About the illustrator

Jane Smith of Chocolate Dog Studio is a full time illustrator who lives in Mapua, near Nelson in New Zealand.

She loves animals and her favourite job is illustrating stories featuring dogs and cats. She enjoys talking to writers about their projects and you can contact her at info@chocolatedog.co.nz

See more of her work at www.chocolatedogillustration.co.nz or follow her on Facebook at Chocolate-Dog-Studio and on Instagram at janesmithillustration